How To Decode Your C
Fortunes

Alice Wickenden

Published by Nine Pens

2022

www.ninepens.co.uk

ISBN: 978-1-7398274-4-1

010

7 orange-peel fortune reader

9 (Well, I'll be damned)

10 Spell

11 An Open Letter to a Road Cleaner

12 11:15 pm.

13 *palomena prasina*

15 Rewatching *Life on Mars*

16 In Cornwall, cabbage whites

17 Ephemera

18 On re-reading Louise Glück's 'Telescope'

19 CONVERSATIONS WITH THE MOON:

AN ESSAY ON POETRY

24 renting aubade

For my friends

orange-peel fortune reader

takes your discarded snakeskin
silently weighs the pith in her hand

you think of Anubis
guarding the underworld:

if your heart is heavier than a feather
Ammit devours it.

a goddess
of lion

hippopotamus
and crocodile

how could she not be starving?
your sin is menial

but she sees it in the way
you treat the fruit.

eat up she says eventually,
with the voice of one who knows your future

and you bite down.
burst of fragrant juice –

(your heart is revealed through small encounters)

(Well, I'll be damned)

Joan Baez in my headphones, rich with
heartbreak, grey air

resounding

and a startled sparrow with its prize of stale bread.
Sickening to think of

time.

The way the blossom comes all at once
like tears,

every year a flood of blush grief.

Spell

By the light of the campfire a single bat
flickers into existence. Unknown to you

before and after. Tissue-paper thing,
halloween-thing, thing ravaged by

the light of the campfire. A group
of bats is a colony or

a cauldron. A group of bats
is nothing to do with you;

a group of bats is a thing
beyond your care;

a group of bats is
gossamer.

Just outside the light
of the campfire:

a group of bats with
unnoticed

eyes.

An Open Letter to a Road Cleaner

Walking down Mile End road I met a dead fox
blood-beaded ; radiant still.

Having never seen a fox so close
alive or not   I stopped.

I had the overwhelming desire
to pick it up   gutspilled

to drape it round my neck and let it red- stain
me instead of the concrete,

which I knew wouldn't remember. The city
wears death so lightly

what is one more creature car-struck?
But I left foxless.

It was gone next time I passed
(imagined maybe):

someone had taken it away.
I don't know whose job that is.

11:15 pm.

Foxes scream outside.
I sit cross-legged by the radiator.

I'm vulnerable to you. I don't know why.
The radiator creaks. Nothing is silent and
I am full of emotions this language has no space for.

One of the foxes has won. Does it matter which? Either way a
rabbit dies.

palomena prasina

There is a great glimmering beetle
crawling ponderously up your arm.

I don't see how anything can stay
clinging on. But he reaches your elbow.

Is it possible for such small feet
to navigate that bend?

Or is my perspective all wrong?
I can't think myself into smallness –

He skipped your fist altogether:
too tricky, too liable to clench.

A bug must learn to pick its fights.
And now —

he has made his way
past the elbow — he is heading to your —

he is on your neck —
he is on your face —

he is squirming
down your mouth and —

whilst you go on talking
green wings jerk helplessly –

pearlescent fragments
splinter down –

and you
haven't noticed a thing.

(I think it was a shield bug:
the air around us is swarming thick.)

Rewatching *Life on Mars*

I'm rewatching *Life on Mars*. The story of a man mad,
dying, or back in time, and we're supposed to wonder which
–

does it matter? He wakes up in a world not his own
and when he tries to point that out no-one understands.

Hey, Sam Tyler, we've all been there, cast adrift
in shirts that don't feel right and a violence you can't control.

In desperate search for meaning. *It's right there, Sam,*
I think, like God. I know what's coming. Spoiler:

you wake up alive and choose to splinter back,
a man who'd rather live in his dreams,

who'd rather jump off the building and die out of the future,
who'd rather hope he might open his eyes again –

and you *do*. You die for joy with joy. And what you wanted
was there
            all along. What meaning am I meant to take from
that?

There's no answer in TV: it's not my leap, Sam.
            When I die I don't wake up.

In Cornwall, cabbage whites

Last night I dreamt I went out of Fowey
along the coastal path. And everywhere I went

were white butterflies, simmering, seething,
refusing my outstretched arm, rejecting stillness.

I wanted to be grown in them like fungi.
A single shifting mass, arms, legs

and antennae. Perhaps then
I could rise into the air –

You never see red butterflies anymore says my dad,
the man who caught and pinned them as a boy,

framed carcasses still heavy in a corner of my
bedroom. I learned to name them like that.

When something wings past I think I hurl a stone
before I know what I am doing. In death

I know it. Soft mangled body underfoot.
I jump a stile: the white field before me lifts shocked,

a ghost of murmured wings.
Implacable they scatter...

Ephemera

(I)

Our third date – the Globe – *King Lear* in the rain.
Ticket stub in my purse and a receipt for two
ponchos. Grizzled grey production and you didn't
know the plot and I tried not to flinch at *a dog a horse*
a rat but still something took my breath away.

(II)

Now you have left all I have is
a bookmark from the place you buy
your books. I feel sick with jealousy:

that there are shops, out there,
with you in them, running your fingers
down their spines, making them

tremble. I let it mark my place &
guide me to where you are: not here
but in the world, not this page

but another. Under no covers but your own.

On re-reading Louise Glück's 'Telescope'

As so often happens, one night
opens out into another.

I think of the June I spent cooped up
in an attic room with slits for windows,

flies for company,
a shapeless undefined feeling. I remember my bed

and the poems of Louise Glück
I kept beside it. How I copied out her promise:

you exist like the stars exist.

I was so unhappy there: the heat of the nights.
I refused to rest until the sun came up,

underlining poems and re-watching films,

sleeping with someone fresh
out of the cocoon of heartbreak,

his blinking tendrils reminding me of how far
I had come.

CONVERSATIONS WITH THE MOON: AN ESSAY ON POETRY

I.

Sylvia Plath, in Cambridge, February 19th 1956, writes:

'So, now I shall talk every night. To myself. To the moon. I shall walk, as I did tonight, jealous of my loneliness, in the blue-silver of the cold moon, shining brilliantly on the drifts of fresh-fallen snow, with the myriad sparkles. … With masks down, I walk, talking to the moon, to the neutral impersonal force that does not hear, but merely accepts my being.'

In 1611, Aemelia Lanyer writes (of the moon):

She deckt her selfe with all the borrowed light
That Phoebus would afford from his faire face.

A woman writing, she knew she could not produce her own light. After all, the moon is only valued for the way it reflects back the sun.

And even then, it is changeable and suspect, it cannot win.

II.

I am deeply sad, I confided to the moon, who was sitting up on her haunches, bored, smoking menthols the same colour as her skin. She blew lazily into the air and shrugged, a *what do you expect me to say* kind of shrug, or perhaps *so what? aren't we all*. We were silent for a while. I had nothing more to say. Sometimes there is no way to expand on sadness; you just have to acknowledge it and I had. The moment hovered.

See you tomorrow, I guess, I said eventually, trying to ignore the overwhelming realisation that there would be a tomorrow. The foreseeable future is so damn long. She nodded, rocking backwards and up into a standing position, stretching out those limbs, briefly vibrant before falling back into glum stillness. I guess, she said.

III.

This is very self-indulgent of you, really. Unoriginal.

What do you mean? That's my *point*. Men, writing about their sadness for centuries, revealing the human soul. I, a woman, dare to take my sadness and put it into — you —

&, she shrugged, amazing how she spoke without words, that symbol resplendent in the flow of her shoulders, that's hardly new, is it? Poets have been projecting onto me for *years*.

I'm not a poet, I said.

No. You're not anything.

They'll call it autobiographical like it's a slur. Look at what happened to Plath. Bleeding over her work, suffering for them, and they sneer: Anyone could do that, live, and write it down.

IV.

I write the letter like my therapist told me to do but I don't
send it or burn it. I want to put it into a bottle and throw it off
the pier. Maybe bury it so it becomes a tree. In the end I put it
in a box out of sight. I lie on my floor in the dark with the
door locked. I think about lying there forever, how slowly or
quickly the house would fall apart, vines and weeds inching
their way, taking it back.

V.

The electric moon flickers on, off, like God pulled the plug,
and she waltzes away, long pale legs. I guess what I'm trying
to say is, there's a sunrise, even if that means being left alone.
I guess what I'm trying to say is, I miss you but it's okay. I
guess what I'm trying to say is, I'll stop thinking about what I
should have said when I said nothing.

renting aubade

Oh, absolutely sinful, birds singing
before it gets light, noises crystallising
in my shitty two-bed alchemical lab

the purpose of which is to dilute &
refract the essence of the city into glimmering
thumping incessant neighbours

& the cat is yowling
because it has the nerve to be 5am
the tendrils of the day stretched to breaking

& fuck it's only Wednesday
all the strength should be sapped from the sheets
but next to me is someone I love, & so – peace.

Acknowledgements

'Spell' was first published in *Cypress Press*. 'Ephemera II' was first published in *Anthropocene*.

Quotes have been taken from Louise Glück, 'Telescope'; the journals of Sylvia Plath, Aemelia Lanyer's 'Salve Deus Rex Judaeorum', William Shakespeare's *King Lear*. The title of 'Well, I'll be Damned' is taken from Joan Baez's song 'Diamonds and Rust'. *Life on Mars* ran on BBC One from 9th January 2006 to 10th April 2007, and holds up remarkably well.

Lightning Source UK Ltd.
Milton Keynes UK
UKHW011240240422
401956UK00001B/36

9 781739 827441